(PLATE ONE)

ON THE COVER: *Hunters in the Snow* (1565)
Kunsthistorisches Museum, Vienna. 46 x 63¾″

Art Treasures of the World

100 SIXTH AVENUE • NEW YORK 13, N. Y.

LANDSCAPE WITH A RABBIT HUNTER (1566). Etching

PIETER

BRUEGEL

THE ELDER

(About 1525-1569)

TEXT BY

WOLFGANG STECHOW

Professor of Fine Arts, Oberlin College

PIETER BRUEGEL'S ART is so universal in scope and so rich in fulfillment that there has not been a period when people wholly ceased to appreciate it. However, this does not mean that all aspects of his greatness have always been equally recognized. From his own time to ours, millions have been delighted by what was considered the "drollness" of his figures and by the unmistakable genuineness of their reactions to the joys and sorrows of life. A generation after Bruegel's death, the Dutch critic and biographer Karel van Mander wrote: "Few are those of his pictures which an onlooker can face without laughing [or] . . . at least smiling." A somewhat similar, though perhaps less naive attitude is still being taken by many modern spectators.

In recent times other grounds for admiration have become more prominent. In the last few decades painters have increasingly stressed matters of form and structure in their interpretation of the outside world, almost to the

THE PAINTER AND THE CONNOISSEUR (about 1565). Pen drawing. Albertina, Vienna

of his activity was spent in making drawings, the earliest of which is dated 1552. In many cases these served as models for professional engravers who during his lifetime made many engravings of allegories, landscapes, ships, etcetera, after his designs (Bruegel himself made only one print, the landscape etching reproduced on page 1). It is safe to say that during his lifetime and for a long period after, Bruegel was best known as designer of such prints rather than as the author of paintings (which few people ever saw); today, on the other hand, the paintings and a few of his drawings have become universally famous through photographic reproductions.

Considering the time and place in which Bruegel lived, and the circumstances under which he was trained, one might have expected that he would become merely another of the many Flemish artists who painted humanistically erudite subjects after the Italian fashion, and Biblical pictures in a style strongly dependent on the heritage of Italian Renaissance art. Bruegel's choice of secular subjects and his treatment of Biblical themes was totally different from theirs, however, and his debt to Italy was very small.

What lasted longest of his southern journey was the impression made by the great mountain ranges of the Alps and of Italy (although their image often fused in his mind and art with the plains of his own country). Also, his Italian studies may have contributed to his sovereign command of compositional tools, and to a sharpened sense of the wholeness of the human body. But otherwise the world of his art is the country in which he lived: its landscape and its people — and of these people, their typical activities, their ever-recurrent sufferings and joys, their ancient traditions, their wisdom and their follies. This holds true even of his pictures with Biblical subjects, because to him, more than to any other artist, the people of the Bible were the people of his own day and of his own country.

As we suggested before, our understanding of Bruegel's specific statements is often hampered by lack of historical knowledge. We do not know with how much exactness Bruegel, clearly a well-educated city-dweller and not a peasant, interpreted the life of the country folk who are the subject of so many of his paintings; how faithfully he followed the generally accepted meaning of proverbs; how much or how little political bias he injected into his work; what the exact sources of his more complicated allegories are. In particular (and contrary to common belief), there is no evidence of his having been the spokesman of a resistance movement against the Spanish rulers of his country.

Fortunately, these gaps in our knowledge are not insurmountable barriers to our understanding of much that is most characteristic in Bruegel's art. He conceived of man not as a free individual, as the Renaissance had done — it is significant that he never painted a portrait — but primarily as dependent on some force of nature, tradition, belief, or rank. Man in Bruegel's pictures acts under compulsion rather than of his own free will. What he does he must do because he is doing it at a certain time of the year or of his life, because he has been trained or

point of eliminating the outside world as a subject of painting; and this could hardly fail to be reflected in our appreciation of even the great "storytellers" and "realists" of the past. Thus, at least in his more mature works, we have discovered a new main facet of Bruegel's greatness: the way in which he subordinated the wealth of his penetrating observations to the needs of artistic organization, practicing selectiveness and restraint for the sake of pictorial clarity.

In fact, the formal aspect of Bruegel's art is now sometimes overstressed, and new efforts are being made to understand both the deeper meaning and the artistic organization of his works, not as two different things but as necessary complements of each other (as we might expect in a truly great artist). Even so, this is still a precarious task, for we are beset by great difficulties in reconstructing the exact nature of Bruegel's own world view. But before touching on this problem let us glance briefly at the little we know about his life and the atmosphere in which he worked.

Pieter Bruegel (or Brueghel), whom we call "the Elder" in order to distinguish him from his son Pieter, a moderately gifted painter, was born about 1525-30 in the vicinity of Breda or of 's-Hertogenbosch (Bois-le-Duc) near the border of present-day Holland and Belgium. In 1551 he became a master in the painters' guild at Antwerp. Soon afterward he went south, and in 1553 he spent some months in Rome, the almost invariable goal of the more ambitious Flemish painters of his day. Probably in 1563 he moved from Antwerp to Brussels, where he died in 1569.

All of his paintings seem to have been done between 1557 and 1568, but we must not forget that a great part taught to do it, or because he is inexorably subject to death, folly, superstition, or other frailties common to men.

Even where he enjoys life he does so as a member of a group; his pleasures are prescribed and unaccompanied by either ease or smiles. This world — which is comparable to that of Bruegel's greatest predecessor, Hieronymus Bosch — may make the spectator laugh, or else send a shiver down his spine as he sees his neighbor and himself characterized as mere spokes in the wheel of life. But even in this dubious world Bruegel discovered one redeeming friend: nature itself. True, man stumbles into the ditch because of bad leadership, turns his back to the world because it cheats him, faces disaster and retribution, works hard for his living, and is prone to unending folly and base indulgence when he is prosperous. But in Bruegel's eyes, nature redeems all this with its radiant and irresistible beauty.

Even though we are uncertain about details of Bruegel's pictures, their whole point is almost invariably evident at once. This wonderful clarity is partly due to his precise design, which he acquired through tireless study of his models (many of his drawings are inscribed *naer het leven,* "from life") and which is supported by "local" colors of strong intensity; it is also due partly to a compositional skill which even in his mature works transcends all purely illustrative considerations. In these, as one critic has said, he "uses a bullet instead of small shot — and hits the bull's eye."

Even the earlier works, which still lack the sublime restraint of the late ones, are still far from being "glorified cartoons." The way in which each group of figures is linked with its neighbor through the interlocking of brilliantly observed bodily movements, as well as through unfailing skill in relating the most complicated three-dimensional poses to the picture plane, elevates even them to the rank of great art; the spectator is led beyond mere "recognition" of a motif to an appreciation of an artistic idea.

The resulting synthesis of meaning and structure which we hinted at earlier will receive individual attention in the commentaries on our plates.

Commentary

COVER (PLATE ONE)
HUNTERS IN THE SNOW (1565)
Kunsthistorisches Museum, Vienna. 46 x 63¾"

THIS GREAT MASTERPIECE belongs to the same series of "The Twelve Months" as *The Harvesters* (plate 9). The challenge to depict a landscape under snow was first realized, and met with amazing skill, by fifteenth-century book illuminators in their renderings of man's activities in February. Bruegel may rather have alluded to December, the more so as he utilized a traditional motif often connected with that month: the preparation of a roast for a festival. But he subordinated this one action to a much more comprehensive view of nature and man in wintertime. Here, nature is familiar — the village roads, plains, trees, ice — but also encompasses foreign wonders — a steep mountain; man returns tired from the day's labors, but also prepares his meal and amuses himself on the skating rink.

Above all, this picture rivals *The Harvesters* in compositional greatness. Space is conquered by the diagonal penetration of trees, huntsmen, and dogs, and extends throughout the vast reaches of middle and background. Those same trees, together with the opposing diagonal formed by the sloping contour of the foreground hill, reaffirm the frontal plane of the picture and establish perfectly that balance and rhythmic order without which even the most wonderful details would create nothing but confusion.

PLATE TWO
THE BATTLE BETWEEN CARNIVAL AND LENT (1559)
Kunsthistorisches Museum, Vienna. 46½ x 65"

THIS IS ONE OF BRUEGEL'S EARLIEST PAINTINGS, characterized by a great accumulation of details in design and color. Every square inch shows us the results of Bruegel's penetrating observation which gives us a magnificent eyeful of Netherlandish everyday life in his time. The subject is allegorical: a translation into visual reality of the tension which occurred annually between the last days of frolicking and the lean Lenten fare and Lenten faces which are about to take over. Bruegel illustrates this contrast in hundreds of different ways. There is an actual fighting match in front (between a fat Prince Carnival mounted on a barrel and a haggard old Lent wielding a shovel with two herrings on it). Innumerable people are having a last fling at fun, play, and good food, while others are coming out of church and performing works of charity. The horizon lies as high as possible in order to accommodate all and sundry.

PLATE THREE
THE TRIUMPH OF DEATH (1560)
The Prado, Madrid. 46⅛ x 63¾"

THIS SOMBER ALLEGORY of the inescapable power of death comes as a shock after Bruegel's earlier gay and genre-like work. At the same time, it may be seen as a harbinger of the greatest of Bruegel's later paintings although it still exhibits the multiplicity of the earlier ones. The medieval concept of Death conquering all ranks of mankind has been preserved: king, cardinal, knights, monks, soldiers, peasants are attacked and defeated alike. But it was Bruegel's own magnificent idea to multiply Death into huge armies of skeletons making shorter work of their victims, who are already compressed into a narrow stratum of the foreground. Also new is a most expressive differentiation between the acceptance of defeat (the slumping cardinal at the left) and last attempts at resistance (the valiant soldier—a lansquenet—at the right). Middle and background are abandoned to other terrors: execution, fires, and shipwreck. The colors are more subdued, the horizon a little lower than before.

PLATE FOUR
Detail of THE TRIUMPH OF DEATH
(upper right corner)
The Prado, Madrid

WHILE ABOUT HALF OF THE PICTURE'S SKY is hidden by fire and smoke, the section shown in this detail is almost clear and, together with the light hues of the water and the beach, throws into relentless relief the scenes of execution assembled on this side. Under a tall wheel, occupied by its victim and an expectant bird of prey, a man in white shirt and blue trousers, crucifix in hand,

ALLEGORY OF HOPE
Engraving after a drawing of 1559,
by Bruegel the Elder

THE BEE-KEEPERS AND THE NEST THIEF
(1565). Pen drawing
Museum, Berlin

is on the point of being beheaded by a huge skeleton. Another is hanged on the gallows with a detachment of skeletons standing at attention. Between more wheels, a bare tree stretches upward, on which a man was impaled long ago. A naked figure hiding in a hollow of the trunk seems to have been pierced with a lance thrown from behind. On the right, a man clad in blue and red may have hoped to escape across the rocks toward the sea, but with lightning speed a skeleton has caught him by the chin from below; grotesquely, the two heads mirror each other as they appear in the upper and lower corners of a diamond formed by bony arms, and down goes the victim in sprawling helplessness.

PLATE FIVE
Detail of THE TRIUMPH OF DEATH
(lower left corner)
The Prado, Madrid

IN THIS DETAIL, THE CARDINAL is collapsing in the arms of a skeleton who mocks him by wearing the hat symbolizing his rank and — more subtly — by aping the outline of his drooping body. At the same time, the emperor, on the extreme left of the picture, indulges in an Italianate pose which combines a concession of defeat with a formal gesture to the observer. Thrown into greater relief by the devilish mimicry of Death hoisting an hourglass, the royal figure points to a kneeling skeleton who gleefully runs his fingers through gold pieces which fill two receptacles, while silver coins are rolling out of another barrel. We recall that in Holbein's *Dance of Death* a point was made of the fact that Death punishes

the miser more cruelly by robbing him of his money than by taking his life.

The two scenes of the cardinal and the emperor are magnificently held together by the weird horizontal motif extending directly and precisely above them. An emaciated mare slowly but steadily drags a carriage over the prostrate forms of several people. Already the carriage is fully laden with skulls which have been scooped together with a big shovel now carelessly dropped on them. One skeleton nonchalantly sits on the vehicle, playing a hurdy-gurdy; another rides sideways on the horse (notice how this seems to retard the tempo of the whole procession), carrying death-bell and lantern, while a raven perched behind him displays an impressive black silhouette before the pallid water.

PLATE SIX
Detail of THE TRIUMPH OF DEATH
(lower right corner)
The Prado, Madrid

THE GAY PARTY IS OVER NOW. On the left, two futile gestures of fighting back with a sword and a bench go almost unnoticed. The only hint at real resistance is embodied in the lansquenet whose resilient silhouette is so magnificently supported by the white table cloth. He is the only human being in the entire picture who is still in a sense "whole," but even here one realizes that his bravado must be short-lived. There is every indication of an effective fifth column behind his back.

While the gambler, frightened out of his wits, seeks refuge

4

under the table, a masked skeleton pours away the wine; others flirt with terrified girls, pretend to serve some weird food, or mockingly accompany the song of a pair of lovers who are happily lost even to this world of terror. And just to make sure that the spectator sees no chance of escape for anyone, a huge reserve army of skeletons approaches from the right middle ground.

PLATE SEVEN
TWO MONKEYS (1562)
Deutsches Museum, Berlin. 7⅞ x 9″

IN THIS TINY PICTURE, two monkeys are chained to a window sill above which we are shown a vista of the city of Antwerp. This bit is one of the most amazing early river views on record, thinly painted in soft grayed tones which foreshadow the art of the Dutch marine painters of the seventeenth century. The foreground of the picture, marked by the artist's characteristic precision, is restricted to subdued tones which contrast, yet harmonize with the distant view by avoiding the bright hues which we know from so many other works of the master.

It is possible that this coloristic restraint was intended to contribute to the expression of gloom conveyed by the two fettered animals which, as has recently been shown, may well symbolize those who have sold their freedom for what a Netherlandish adage calls a "banquet of three hazelnuts." It is even conceivable that by placing this allegory before a view of Antwerp, Bruegel alluded to himself being chained by some unreasonable bond to that city, which in fact he left for good a year or so after he painted this panel. However this may be, the beauty of that enchanting view must have been as decisive a factor in the making of the picture as it still is in our appreciation of it.

PLATE EIGHT
THE ADORATION OF THE MAGI (1564)
The National Gallery, London. 43½ x 32½″

BRUEGEL PAINTED ONLY A FEW PICTURES in upright format, and it is fascinating to see how this choice affected the entire character of such a work. It eliminated the narrative, almost talkative, mood of an earlier representation of the same subject with its crowds of people pleasantly spread over its horizontal surface, and made the painter concentrate on the more selective method of composing with relatively few figures — which eventually led to the superb simplicity of his last works. Reminiscences from Flemish paintings of the fifteenth century seem to have been combined with influences from later Italian altarpieces, in which this format and general arrangement were frequently used.

The characterization of the actors, however, has no parallel anywhere in the history of painting, not even in the similarly unconventional casts of Hieronymus Bosch, Bruegel's great Netherlandish forerunner. The spectators of the scene, simple people from the retinue of the Magi, are all agape at the unexpected scene of the adoration of the little peasant child. There are even some irreverent suggestions being whispered into Joseph's ear by a local gossip, and the Moorish King Balthasar himself looks flabbergasted rather than inspired. But the main group, with the wonderfully sincere devotion of the two older kings and Mary's slightly embarrassed yet gracious response, would not impress us so deeply but for the circle of reverent or astonished onlookers.

PLATE NINE
THE HARVESTERS (1565)
The Metropolitan Museum of Art, New York. 46½ x 63¼″

TOGETHER WITH FOUR OTHER KNOWN WORKS, this belongs to a

series of paintings which originally numbered (or was intended to number) twelve, and represented "The Twelve Months." The artist is still linked to a medieval tradition which considers the life of man in terms of typical aspects defined by his dependence upon seasons and months. In late medieval calendars the "Labors of the Months" appeared as book illuminations, in which lively characterizations of the seasonal aspects of nature had already occurred.

The greatness of Bruegel's *Harvesters*, which probably represents July, lies not only in the freshness of observation which has been lavished on its middle and background; even more significant is the power of the magnificent tree which serves as a backbone to the entire composition and as a center toward which the group of eating, drinking, and resting laborers is magnetically drawn. But the scent of midsummer which permeates the picture rises from the great central mass of wheat, which dominates its scattered tributaries, dwarfs the men who are working near it and, with its unimpaired yellowness, brilliantly epitomizes the breath-taking fecundity of the season.

PLATE TEN
THE WEDDING DANCE (1566)
The Detroit Institute of Arts, Michigan. 47 x 62″

BRUEGEL, IN THIS PICTURE, decided to emphasize the accompanying circumstances of an event rather than the event itself. The characterization of a Flemish peasant dance became more important to him than the wedding which occasioned it. Indeed, at first glance, we could almost be forgiven for doubting the presence of a bride and groom. But in the far distance we can discover the bride's crown, which still hangs on a screen above her former seat. The bride herself is the redhaired girl to the left of the center who wears a wreath on her head which sets her off from the other women with their white headdresses. Holding her hand is the groom, who occupies the exact center of the composition. Otherwise, the picture is all dance rhythm, with the foreground pairs swinging freely between the post-like figures of the bagpipe player on the right and the onlooker on the left.

PLATE ELEVEN
THE MASSACRE OF THE INNOCENTS (1566)
Kunsthistorisches Museum, Vienna. 43¾ x 63″

THE TERRIFYING BIBLICAL STORY has been sublimated into a terrifying story from all ages which knew — and still know — war, pillage, and the killing of innocent children. Specifically, it has become a story of Bruegel's own era. But it would be wrong to conclude from this that he aimed the picture at the Spanish soldiery then stationed in Flanders: to him, *all* stories from the Bible were events of his own time.

The wholesale murder ordered by Herod is depicted as a winter scene because it happened just after the birth of Christ. A snowfall has blanketed the peaceful Flemish village which has suddenly become a place of random slaying, desperate but fruitless pleas and forlorn wails over torn little bodies. Houses are broken into and searched for more victims as a phalanx of mailed horsemen seals off the middle ground with terrible finality. Beyond, there are only silenced houses, bare trees, and a leaden winter sky.

PLATE TWELVE
THE CONVERSION OF SAUL (1567)
Kunsthistorisches Museum, Vienna. 42½ x 61½″

ONCE AGAIN, BRUEGEL HAS SLIGHTED THE MAIN THEME, in comparison with his treatment of the accompanying details. But while in other cases he did so for the sake of depicting Flemish landscapes or scenes of everyday life, his chief inspiration for this painting originated in the grandeur of an Alpine view. Bruegel remembered the wild beauty of one of the mountain passes to Italy, which he had traveled fifteen years before, as he painted the road to Damascus on which Saul was smitten, blinded, and converted by the voice of the Lord, to become Paul.

The mountain landscape, however, is the real hero of the picture. For visionary power it has few peers even among Bruegel's own interpretations of nature. Horsemen and footsoldiers alike seem to have become part of the great terrestrial force which drives cliffs and trees upward with passionate abandon, up toward the spot where Saul lies helpless before his horse, his disturbed companions, and a threatening wall of dark fir trees, and further up still toward the cloud-invested pass where human forms are absorbed into nature's infinity.

PLATE THIRTEEN
THE LAND OF COCKAYNE (1567)
Bavarian State Collections, Munich. 20½ x 30¾"

BRUEGEL HAS CONJURED UP some of the greatest visions of folk legends that have ever been imagined, and ennobled them through an artistic organization which transcends mere illustration or "quotation." In this superb depiction of the land of overflowing plenty, mankind is still seen in terms of various ranks which, taken together, stand for "everyone." Soldier, peasant, and clerk are each characterized by his costume and by an appropriate attribute: lance, threshing flails, writing utensils; and they have become the spokes of that weird wheel of laziness and gluttony which has stopped rotating for want of momentum. The bellies, backs, legs, heads, table, egg, pancakes — all are round; and so is the very piece of earth on which everything and everyone weighs down relentlessly. A round human form is heavily descending from a round hole in the round "riceberg" in the background. There is no air, no relief from stuffing anywhere; the full stomach reigns supreme and as though for eternity.

PLATE FOURTEEN
THE BIRD'S NEST (1568)
Kunsthistorisches Museum, Vienna. 23¼ x 26¾"

THIS ENCHANTING PICTURE COMBINES some pointed irony with a great serenity which is reflected in its fresh, and gay colors. The proverb on which part of its meaning is based suggests the same combination of qualities. In a friendly jingle it comments that "he who knows where the nest is, knows it; he who takes it, owns it."

But Bruegel has also something else in mind. The peasant in the foreground knows where the nest is and could easily get it; far from threatening the boy who robs it he seems to indicate that

the boy acts foolishly in risking his neck. Yet although at first glance his powerful form suggests security, a closer look reveals that a rude shock is in store for him. He is walking straight into a pond which he has overlooked in his gay complacency. Though he thinks he is so clever, he is the fool, after all. While disparaging the boy's determination, he ends up by being "all wet." But this must not be taken too seriously; the bright beauty of the landscape (whose horizon is now quite low) outshines everything.

PLATE FIFTEEN
THE BEGGARS (1568)
The Louvre, Paris. 7 x 8¼"

GROUPS OF CRIPPLES AND BEGGARS held a great fascination for Bruegel, whose forthright rendering of their grotesque misery foreshadows Callot and Rembrandt. It is hard for us to imagine the impression which such pictures must have made on his not-too-priggish contemporaries: probably the same kind of strange mixture of amusement and spine-tingling as children may experience before sights of this kind. However that may be, this extraordinary small panel is distinguished by a composition of almost frightening monumentality. The two brick walls left and right, and the opening in the center with the distant gateway, together with the carefully calculated structure of the main group, lend to these unlucky fragments of humanity a dignity and even grandeur. The broad modeling of their forms suggests the knife of a woodcutter, applied to human blocks that are endowed with a remarkable weather resistance. These wrecks will outlast many whole men of more delicate fiber.

PLATE SIXTEEN
THE PEASANT WEDDING (1568)
Kunsthistorisches Museum, Vienna. 45 x 64½"

ONE OF BRUEGEL'S RARE INTERIOR SCENES, this picture vies with the *Wedding Dance* (plate 10) in simplicity and monumentality, while yet containing a wonderful variety of characters. The main subject is once more somewhat slighted. The bride, although distinguished by curtain and crown, is relegated to the center of the background area amidst her parents, a benign aristocratic visitor, and the other guests. The groom (in the center, clad in black) is so inconspicuous that sometimes the presence of this major actor in the scene has been overlooked. All are overtowered by the huge figures of the purveyors who, sharply emphasized by the brilliant, unbroken colors of their garments, tramp across the right front with their golden provisions, sharing compositional honors with the musicians, the dispenser of drinks, and a child completely depersonalized by self-indulgence. A few basic lines — an obtuse angle, a diagonal, a horizontal, and some short verticals — hold all this wealth firmly together.

THE TITLE, SIZE, AND OTHER PERTINENT DATA ON THE PAINTINGS THAT FOLLOW
WILL BE FOUND BY LIFTING EACH REPRODUCTION

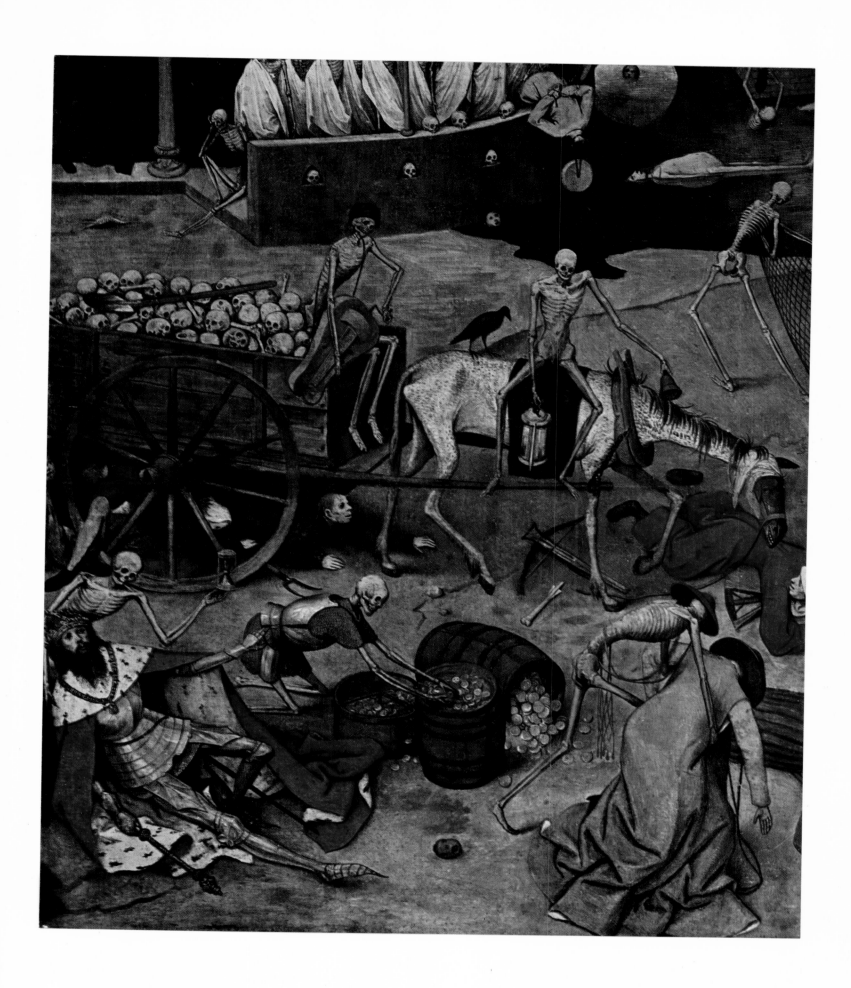

ON THE COVER
THE GARDEN OF WORLDLY DELIGHTS
RIGHT WING: Detail of *Hell*. The Prado, Madrid
(see commentary for plate 12)

MILTON S. FOX, Editor

Art Treasures of the World
100 SIXTH AVENUE · NEW YORK 13, N. Y.

THE TEMPTATION OF ST. ANTHONY. Central panel: 51¼ x 46⅞"; Wings: 51¼ x 20".

National Museum of Fine Arts, Lisbon

HIERONYMUS

Bosch

(About 1450-1516)

Text by

LOTTE BRAND PHILIP

THE PAINTINGS BY Hieronymus Bosch have a special and vivid interest for the art loving public of our time, an interest which far exceeds esthetic appreciation. Modern man is inclined to see in them such close and intrinsic relations to his own ideas that he is often tempted to look at these works in the same way that he looks at contemporary art. Yet the painter who created them lived at the end of the Middle Ages in a spiritual climate quite different from the one of our time.

Little is known about the life of Bosch. He was born about 1450 in 's-Hertogenbosch (Bois-le-Duc), a town in North Brabant which now belongs to Holland. He married, lived, and worked in this town, and he died there in 1516. His real name was Van Aeken; Bosch is a surname derived from the name of his birthplace. It is true that 's-Hertogenbosch was not one of the great art centers of the time; on the other hand, it was not exactly provincial either, the town's church of St. John being one of the proudest and most imposing late medieval cathedrals of the Netherlands. The master was the esteemed and well-to-do owner of a flourishing workshop, and he was a member of a highly respectable religious brotherhood, the

1

the new worldly tendencies. The actual—though sometimes not the obvious—subject of all of Bosch's paintings is the world. His entire interest is concentrated on this theme, a completely new one in altar-painting. The world, however, which Bosch depicts is not the world as we see it today. Not even the term "world" had the same meaning as it has in our time. "World" did not as yet mean the more or less neutral abode of good as well as evil. To Bosch the word still had its old biblical connotation signifying the realm which is opposed to the Kingdom of Heaven and which as such must be evil throughout. It is the devilish world which surrounds his saints and hermits, continuing to trouble and tempt them even as they flee it. It is this world which is symbolized in the figures of diabolic executioners torturing a helpless Christ. It is this world and its vices which is represented in the central panel of the so-called *Garden of Worldly Delights* in a complicated metaphor, still enigmatic in most of its details but entirely clear in its basic meaning. To Bosch the world was firmly in the grip of the devil and his demonic helpers, mankind having the barest chance of escape.

In the two large altarpieces which most clearly demonstrate his pessimistic philosophy, the *Hay-Wain* and the *Garden of Worldly Delights,* the way of man categorically goes from earthly paradise via the world to hell. There is not the slightest indication of the comforting possibility of a Heavenly Paradise for any soul. This, of course, is also the result of the moralizing and didactic tendencies of his time. He holds up a mirror to a world full of vices and shows the individual punishments for each of them in the systematically applied tortures of an organized inferno.

However, it is Bosch's specific way of depicting his ideas which has established his fame during all the following centuries and which is the reason for the particular fascination his art holds for us now. Bosch very rarely says things directly. To represent the elements constituting his "world" and his hell, he prefers to speak in symbols and metaphors of his own invention or, at times, at least of his own clever combination. He creates complicated and puzzling configurations by fusing ideas taken from different contexts and shaping them into one single, visible symbol. Or he takes the text of a proverb or biblical passage and depicts the symbolic wording literally.

His methods of transformation and combination vary; his imagination is inexhaustible. The result is a fascinating world of monstrous formations, full of wit and surprises, double and triple meanings, and the eternal magic of the hide-and-seek of ideas. The educated spectator of his time who was still familiar with the sources Bosch used to form his symbols, and who knew the various contexts from which this material was drawn, must have taken great delight in deciphering the artist's brilliant concoctions. This was undoubtedly also the fascination which the paintings held for Philip II of Spain, the "Catholic King," austere persecutor of heresy, who was a great admirer of Bosch. A large number of the painter's works which have come down to us originally formed part of the King's art collection. Philip, as an erudite man who lived in a period still close to Bosch's own life was doubtless capable of deciphering the meaning of the paintings without "research."

To the modern spectator, however, who has lost the knowledge of Bosch's sources, most of the painter's symbolic representations have become completely enigmatic. He nevertheless looks at them with great pleasure and not only because to him they have the charm of abstruse-

Confraternity of Our Lady. Although most of the commissions he received seem to have been given to him by wealthy burghers, there is documentary proof that he painted an altarpiece—a Last Judgment—for a princely patron, Philip the Fair, in 1504. Most of the paintings by Hieronymus Bosch which have come down to us, very probably all of them, are altarpieces or fragments thereof. Some of them bear his characteristic signature which his imitators often copied, because works in his manner were much in demand. None of his paintings is dated.

The known facts of the life of Bosch as well as his work itself give evidence that he was a true believer in the Catholic faith. While, because of the strange character of his art, some critics have thought that Bosch was a heretic, there can hardly be any doubt that all of his paintings were created in and for the service of the great, universal, spiritual power of his time, the Church, which was then still ruling the entire life of European man. Yet this was the period immediately preceeding the Reformation, a time of profound perturbation of the human mind. A new era with strong worldly tendencies had emerged. Medieval man, incapable as yet of coping spiritually with these new trends, regarded himself as entangled in sin and unable to see his way to Salvation. The result was a frantic dread of the devil and of hell, and a violent fear of eternal damnation. The Church in a desperate attempt to check the new worldliness did much to aggravate this fear. She again and again pointed out the sins and vices of man, using eternal damnation as a threat to induce mankind to renounce their evil ways.

The paintings by Hieronymus Bosch mirror this specific attitude of the Church. Curiously enough, they also reflect ness. He sees in them something very close to his own dream symbols and, indeed, there is more than a superficial similarity between the two. Both are unreal but similar enough to nature to be frightfully convincing, and both are the result of an intricate modifying process of the mind. There is yet another and very important function both share: they are both powerfully effective in conveying the feeling for the thing they seek to hide and which reveals itself only through careful interpretation. The elusive quality of Bosch's paintings need not be an obstacle to the enjoyment of the art lover of today. Even without detailed knowledge of their precise significance, he may subconsciously grasp their essential meaning and thereby gain access to their esthetic quality.

The work of Hieronymus Bosch is very beautiful. The jewellike surfaces of Bosch's panels, his technical virtuosity and his color schemes, displayed in limitless variety, are a delight in themselves. In his sublime landscapes full of seductive charm, in his night scenes with their melancholy water expanses and their fabulous conflagrations, in his extraordinary representations of strange forms borrowed seemingly at random from the animal, plant, and mineral kingdoms, he has created a beauty never achieved before and hardly ever surpassed after. Although he states time and again that the world is evil, he cannot help saying that it is beautiful and that its sins and vices, to say the least, are very interesting. In fact, he has created, surely against his own intentions, something which has been called an apotheosis of evil. However, it could just as well be called an apotheosis of nature, for Bosch was not only one of its finest observers, he was also what may be called an initiate of its mysteries. He knew how nature works. We might well ask if the increasing popularity which Hieronymus Bosch has enjoyed in the last generation is not a sign of the inner affinity between his age and ours, each period in its own way having been shocked into the awareness of the demoniacal powers inherent in nature.

Commentary *by Lotte Brand Philip*
(NOTE: *commentaries 1 and 16 are by the editorial staff.*)

1 THE ADORATION OF THE MAGI
Oil and tempera on panel. 28 x 22¼"
The Metropolitan Museum of Art, New York

THIS CHARMING PAINTING is a typical Adoration scene: the Virgin and Child sit enthroned in the center; the elderly Joseph kneels at the left; the three kings, magnificently clothed and carrying splendid gifts, stand in a group at the right. The ox and ass can be seen through the arch at the left behind Joseph, and the shepherds lean over a sill, one warming his hands at a convenient fire toward the rear of the dilapidated, castle-like building.

Scholars believe through observation of the color scheme, the figure style, and the perspective, that this painting is a youthful work in the tradition of early Dutch masters. The delicate hues and the somewhat stiff, rather flat and weightless figures are characteristic of that period of his development. The painting has no middle distance, but only the foreground space of the room, and the faraway landscape. This and the placement of the canopy held by angels, presumably over the heads of the Virgin and Child and yet at the same time over architectural members that are well behind her, show a confusion in the understanding of perspective which could be attributed to an early work.

On the other hand some qualities of Bosch's mature style are already evident. Some scholars believe that it actually reflects later works. Everything is painted with meticulous detail: the Virgin's hair, the pattern on the brocade of the King's robe, the straw on the floor, the bird's nest in a tiny window of the tower. His careful study of facial types begins even here to approach the caricature style he used so often later (see plate 3). The strange, unearthly quality, here still sweet and tender, becomes in later paintings weird, fantastic, and terrifying.

2 CHRIST CROWNED WITH THORNS
Oil and tempera on panel. 29 x 23¼"
National Gallery, London

THIS UNTRADITIONAL REPRESENTATION of the Crowning with Thorns depicts the scene in a rather flat pattern of large heads and hands against a neutral background. The picture, with its almost regular grouping of four heads around the face of the Saviour, does not merely represent an incident from the Passion but has a more universal meaning, as it shows the demonic world opposed to the Kingdom of Heaven.

Christ's torturers are distinctly characterized as the representatives of this world, not only by their facial expression, but by their symbols as well. The man at the lower left, for instance, wears a half moon on his headdress. This is the sign of Islam which to the Middle Ages stood for heresy in general. The turban of the torturer at the upper left is pierced by an arrow, a symbol which in Bosch's paintings quite often stands for eternal death. The man at the upper right wears a bunch of oak leaves on his hat. The oak is a tree which was venerated in pagan cults and which, even in biblical passages, appears as a symbol of paganism. In Bosch's painting the oak leaves seem also to make a special allusion to the custom of wearing green leaves during the Easter season. This heathen custom, which was derived from pre-Christian spring rituals, has survived in many parts of Europe up to our time.

The four faces, moreover, are characterized as four distinctly different types. To the medieval mind there were four different kinds of man which together formed the picture of the whole of mankind. Here the four evil faces undoubtedly symbolize the entirety of a demonic world in a fashion reminiscent of representations in late medieval graphic art with the four humors surrounding the face of God.

Christ in the center of the four figures addresses the spectator with a look of deep sadness, as though to say: Behold, what the wicked ones are doing to me. Fight the sins and vices in your own soul and renounce the evil ways of a demonic world.

3 THE EPIPHANY
Oil and tempera on panel
CENTRAL PANEL: 53¾ x 28⅞"; WINGS: 53¾ x 13¼"
The Prado, Madrid

ACCORDING TO CHRISTIAN TRADITION the three Magi who have come to pay homage to the new-born Messiah are kings from three different parts of the world. To the Middle Ages, they were the representatives of the three continents known at that time, Europe, Asia, and Africa, and as such were symbols of the entire world. Representations of the Adoration of the Magi were often used as the central theme of altarpieces in order to show Christ as the "King of Kings" and to symbolize the triumph of His Kingdom over the world.

In his solemn act of Adoration, Bosch has expressed the same idea. His representation has, nevertheless, a deeply equivocal character reflecting his pessimistic view of the "world." In the large, encyclopedic landscape as well as in the area of the tumble-down stable, various frightening, demonic machinations are represented as symbols of the powers of evil and of the multiple temptation confronting a world just about to worship the Divine Child.

3

4 Detail of THE EPIPHANY
Oil and tempera on panel
The Prado, Madrid

FROM THE DOOR of the ruinous stable, between the pompous figure of the Moorish King and his two kneeling companions, a strange and spectacular half-nude figure emerges. This is the Antichrist who, according to an old and now completely forgotten Christian tradition, is the false Jewish Messiah who will appear at the end of time, shortly before the Last Judgment, to seduce the kings of the world to evil. He holds the kneeling King's helmet which is turned upside down, thus forming a funnel which according to Dante's description was the shape of hell. In the other opening of the hut the over-large head of a donkey is visible. While the ass is an animal traditional in pictures of the Epiphany where it appears together with the ox, Bosch has represented the donkey alone, shaping him into another demonic symbol. He depicts only the donkey's head which, according to one of the oldest calumnies against Judaism, was adored by the Jews in their temple. The animal head and the Antichrist thus form a diabolic ensemble. It is the false ass-idol and its wicked priest which Bosch uses as symbols of heresy and temptation. At the top of the hut, above the head of the false Messiah, rotting roofing-felt and a bunch of straw with long ends coming down like rays, form a fake heaven and a fake star in mocking contrast to the real sky with the star of Bethlehem, the star of the true Saviour, which appears in bright, cloudless beauty above the city of Jerusalem (See plate 3. In the detail, only the rays of the false star are visible).

5 THE GARDEN OF WORLDLY DELIGHTS
LEFT WING: *Earthly Paradise*
Oil and tempera on panel. 86⅝ x 38¼″
The Prado, Madrid

WITH THIS REPRESENTATION, the drama of the largest and most important work by Bosch starts to unfold. As a sort of prelude to the drama, the *Creation of the World* is shown on the outside of this altarpiece and is visible when the wings are closed. When they are opened, this panel at the left showing the Creation of Eve in a fantastic landscape of the Earthly Paradise marks the beginning of the story of man.

The landscape with its high horizon is divided into several planes. The upper plane shows in the light blue hues of a far distance strange, dream-like stone and plant formations, reminders of the ancient aspect of a still uninhabited earth. They are, however, already populated by birds, as the entire landscape unfolding lower down shows the Earthly Paradise after the creation of the animals. This upper plane gradually merges into one of brownish and greenish shades with a similar fantastic structure of nature, towerlike and penetrated by openings forming the passage for a superbly painted arabesque of flying birds. Still further below, the landscape is interlaced with water and animated with all kinds of animals, some fantastic and "prehistoric" and some of them exotic. The unicorn on the left is just about to dip his horn into the water to purify it so that the other animals may drink. On a little island where pearls and precious stones have accumulated, a pink, fairytale structure, the Fountain of Life, sending down thin sprays of water, marks the center of the Earthly Paradise.

6 THE GARDEN OF WORLDLY DELIGHTS
LEFT WING: Detail of *Earthly Paradise*
Oil and tempera on panel
The Prado, Madrid

THE LOWER PART of the wing shows the *Creation of Eve*. Three large figures are placed on a sloping lawn of the garden which ends with a pond in the right foreground. The Creator standing in the center of the group and looking at the spectator holds the newly created Eve by the hand. With eyes modestly downcast, she kneels on a grassy hillock, her slim figure silhouetted against a veil of golden hair. Her future spouse sitting at the left on the grass gazes at her in wonderment. The small rabbit behind her is a fertility symbol prophetic of her role as the future mother of mankind.

Behind the group stretches the orchard of the Garden of Eden with lovely, red, ripe apples. At the left, next to Adam, a magnificent, exotic tree lifts its palm-like branches upwards. A bizarre berry-carrying parasite climbs up it in graceful curves. In Bosch's conception, these poisonous looking berries, and not the apples, seem to be the forbidden fruits of the garden.

The lawn and the pond swarm with all kinds of creatures in which Bosch appears to have given a first indication of the possibility of evil. The cat has already caught a mouse, and a broad-beaked bird has hunted a frog. The queer heron with three heads and the other monstrosities do not seem to be just "prehistoric" but of downright evil nature.

7 THE GARDEN OF WORLDLY DELIGHTS
Oil and tempera on panel. CENTRAL PANEL: 86⅝ x 76¾″
The Prado, Madrid

SINCE THE SCENES of the left wing close with the *Creation of Eve* and do not include any of the subsequent chapters from the story of the first couple, it seems very probable that the center part of the altarpiece shows the result of the creation of woman. Bosch does not actually depict the biblical story which recounts that Adam and Eve ate the forbidden fruit, the incident known as the Fall of Man which traditionally symbolizes the beginning of the sex life of mankind. But he implies this idea as he represents the continuous repetition of the Fall of Man ever after on earth.

The scenery of his painting unfolds like a huge map of the world. The four fantastic structures at the upper plane signify the four corners of the world, and the four streams of water flowing toward them are the four rivers of the earth which are thought to have sprung from the Earthly Paradise. Yet, in Bosch's painting, their origin is not the paradisiac fountain. It is a new worldly version of the Fountain of Life which stands in the center of the water that connects the four corners of the world. This fountain holds a specific symbolism.

Since life on earth has its origin in the relations of the sexes, this new earthly fountain is a symbol of these relations. It might be called the "Fountain of Lust." The behavior of the nude couples who populate the structure does not leave any doubt about its character. What is symbolized here as well as in the picture as a whole is the longing and desire of the sexes and their eternal lusts and delights. In other words, it is exactly the realm which the Middle Ages thought to be ruled by the sin of *luxuria* (lust). In fact, this altarpiece, in one of the old sources, has actually been called *Luxuria*.

Yet, in the belief of the Middle Ages, all sins and vices are interwoven and one derives from the other. Therefore, it is not only *luxuria* which is depicted here but all the sins brought forth by this vice and all the vices which cause *luxuria*. This is quite evident in the right wing which, in a horrifying inferno, presents the punishment of all kinds of sins.

8 THE GARDEN OF WORLDLY DELIGHTS
Oil and tempera on panel. Detail of CENTRAL PANEL
The Prado, Madrid

THE LIGHT GREEN LAWN and the quiet blue water of the foreground swarm with groups of nude male and female figures. Fruits, plants, and various animals, birds, and fish, some frighteningly oversize, form part of the composition of each group. Two large, pink, ball-shaped fruit shells are floating on the water. Their fantastic spheres combined with, or gracefully developing into, other plant formations, serve as vehicles for the human figures. From the fruit shell at the left, leaves of the same pink color grow out in charming curves, developing into the stem of a fantastic flower. A huge bubble of organic character emanates from the flower. Inside this transparent sphere an amorous couple engage in tender love-making. They are a picture of sweet and gentle affection. The sinful nature of their behavior, however, is undoubtedly indicated by the symbols underneath. The mouse always signifies evil.

Groups engaged in various occupations of an obvious sexual

nature fill the picture everywhere. A man carries an amorous couple in an oversized oyster shell. A huge blackberry floating on the water is attacked by a circle of men partly submerged in the water. A picture of hungry and ardent desire, they strive anxiously to get their share. The eating of fruit, unquestionably a symbol of the Fall of Man derived from the biblical story, is a motive which again and again is repeated all over the painting. Also, in popular sayings of all nations, fruits of various kinds play an important part as symbols of sex. The same is true of animals and fish, and especially of birds. It seems likely that in some of these symbolic groups Bosch has literally depicted expressions used in the everyday language of his time.

9   THE GARDEN OF WORLDLY DELIGHTS
Oil and tempera on panel. Detail of CENTRAL PANEL
The Prado, Madrid

ON THE RIGHT SIDE of the foreground the representation of the symbolic groups continues in the same fashion. Nude figures in combination with large animals or fruits, or emerging from fantastic structures, or enclosed in a coral-like formation, or in a transparent bell, are engaged in symbolic performances. In one case it is possible to point out the meaning of their doings at least partly. The two men at the left, one picking lilies from the other's buttocks, doubtlessly represent a pun in French and Latin. A similar representation in an emblem book gives evidence that this means "au cul lis," the sound of the French words suggesting the Latin "oculis," a case of the noun meaning "eyes." In the emblem the word forms part of the sentence "habe mortem prae oculis" (keep death before your eyes); here, however, the strange behavior of the group probably refers in some way to the lust of the eyes.

This example clearly illustrates the method of Bosch's representations. Although the group is engaged in a strictly symbolical action which in itself is not obscene at all, the very sight of it suggests the essential sexual meaning of the saying illustrated through it.

In the center of this detail we see the figure of a negress. She is only one of the many graceful, black figures which are interspersed among the beautiful, slender, white nudes throughout the entire painting. This combination may signify not only that *luxuria* is the vice of all races but may also have something to do with old pre-Christian magic tales and verses which have survived in some parts of Europe up to our time. In the demonic and sexual machinations recounted in these verses, the variation of white and black figures plays an important part. Since to Bosch nature and sex are demonic and evil, he might very well have referred to ancient pagan demonology.

10   THE GARDEN OF WORLDLY DELIGHTS
Oil and tempera on panel. Detail of CENTRAL PANEL
The Prado, Madrid

IN THIS MIDDLE PART of the central panel male figures on various mounts are circling around a pool in which female figures are bathing. The large circle of animals is obviously meant as a symbol of the zodiac, though none of the actual zodiac signs, like Aries, Taurus, Gemini, etc., is depicted. Bosch has again taken a word and has represented its meaning literally. Since the Dutch word for zodiac is *dierenriem* (cycle of animals) the painter has merely represented a circle of various beasts. The zodiac is a traditional representation and symbolizes the temporal character of earthly life in contrast to the timelessness of eternal life in Heaven. Thus Bosch has included the zodiac as an indispensable element in his huge map of the world. By depicting the term literally he is able to give his representation still another meaning. The animals symbolize the various sins, vehicles for human lust. Some of the creatures are identical with those represented on the left wing and which there also have shown an evil character. Riders and animals circling around the pool symbolize male desire; the pool itself with its black and white bathing beauties, demonic female seduction. Bosch's circle of animals has a meaning much more specific than a normal circle of zodiac signs which would symbolize simply the perpetual repetition of the periods of the year. His animals and their riders revolving around the pool picture the

continuous repetition in nature wrought by its demonic, procreative forces.

11   THE GARDEN OF WORLDLY DELIGHTS
RIGHT WING: *Hell*
Oil and tempera on panel. 86⅝ x 38¼″
The Prado, Madrid

THE DRAMA OF MAN CLOSES with a terrifying night scene painted in dark and glowing colors. The sweetness of sin is followed by the horrors of punishment. Like the landscape of the other two panels, the scenery of hell is divided into several planes, one merging into the other. Each plane is crowded with groups signifying the individual punishments for a particular sin. Although Bosch seems to have followed neither the concept of the Seven Deadly Sins nor the older system of the eight vices, all the traditional sins are clearly recognizable. There are eight groups which stand out distinctly, four of them on the lower plane of the landscape.

The group at the lower left shows people who have wasted their time in shallow diversions instead of having worked for the salvation of their souls. All requisites of the tavern—table, wine jugs, playing cards, dice, and other games—are depicted, and the scene looks like the tumultuous and unhappy ending of a hilarious party. Above, at the left, musical instruments turned into instruments of torture mark the realm of *luxuria* (lust). At the right, a soul-eating bird-devil is enthroned on a fancy night-stool. At his feet the beautiful, vain girl in the embrace of a beastly lover sits in front of a devilish mirror suggesting that the group shows the punishment of *superbia* (pride). At the lower right, a sow in nun's habit makes love to a male who seems to be a legacy hunter, judging from the accessories of ink-well, documents, and seals. This group possibly signifies *avaritia* (avarice).

It is interesting that not only *luxuria* as such, but also all the other groups relate in one way or another to the sin of lust. This is not surprising since the middle panel presents *luxuria* as its basic theme.

ON THE COVER
12   THE GARDEN OF WORLDLY DELIGHTS
RIGHT WING: Detail of *Hell*
Oil and tempera on panel
The Prado, Madrid

A RIVER LANDSCAPE gruesomely illuminated by various conflagrations is represented at the top of this fantastic picture of hell. Sparks and debris erupting from the fires fill the cloudy sky of the horrible night.

Below are four more groups depicting the punishment of sins. The group at the lower left is very probably meant to be *acedia* (sloth). It shows the punishment of people who have been too lazy to go to church. Negligence in spiritual matters is the oldest concept of this vice. The representation at the right seems to be the punishment of *ira* (wrath). The two large ears pierced by an arrow and holding a knife have recently been identified as *invidia* (envy).

The famous monster in the center standing in the icy water of hell is a symbol of *gula* (gluttony). His body is a large, empty egg shell which is pierced by the bare branches of his tree-like legs. His torso also resembles a carcass, the loathsome remains of a heavy meal. Inside the body a group of unfortunate souls sitting stiff, benumbed with horror, and obviously unable to eat or drink, are being served by a devilish hostess. The white, corpse-like head of the monster wears a huge hat made of a pink bagpipe with a table forming its brim. Condemned souls led by demonic escorts circle around on the table in a gruesome, after-dinner walk. The sinking ships which form the feet of the monster are also symbols of *gula*. In a fifteenth-century source *gula* is compared to the tempest of the seas which overthrows ships and the men in them.

The prominent place given to gluttony in this picture of hell can be explained by the basic theme of the altarpiece. According to an old tradition it was *gula* which induced man to eat the forbidden fruit in Paradise, which caused the Fall of Man and which is the root of *luxuria*.

5

13 THE HAY-WAIN

Oil and tempera on panel. 53⅛ x 39⅝″
The Prado, Madrid

THE FUTILITY OF WORLDLY LIFE is here represented in the simple allegory of a harvest festival. A wagon moves from left to right in front of a cosmic landscape, as if to illustrate the fleeting character of all earthly life, while some exponents of the deadly sins, thinly disguised as *tableaux vivants* which we might encounter at a village fair, occupy the foreground. The wagon is loaded with a large bulk of hay, symbol of the worthless goods of the world. This symbol, ultimately derived from biblical passages, occurs in various proverbs like "all is hay" or "the world is a haystack." The people surrounding the wagon are the entirety of mankind unable to recognize the spiritual worthlessness of all worldly "values." The group between the wheels is desperately attemping to pull bushels of hay from the wagon. They fall into fights over it, are run over by the wagon and become entangled in all kinds of sins, misfortunes, and even murder, while trying to "make hay." At the left a nun with her lover resting at her knees and with her illegitimate child in her arms sits in front of a group to whom a false prophet is preaching "the gospel of hay." Pope, emperor, and princes are following the wagon as their thoughts are likewise directed toward the world and its goods. All sins and follies can be found in this painting. *Luxuria* again holds a prominent place among them. This sin is represented by the embracing couple in the bush on top of the hay-wain, and by the musical group in front of them. These are the merry and careless people who are "on top of the world." They are shown between devil and angel. The demon accompanies their music on his infernal flute, whereas the angel who looks up to Christ appearing in the sunny clouds prays for the salvation of their souls. Yet we realize that he prays in vain since a horde of monsters pulls the wagon with all its people right into the horrors of hell which are represented on the right wing of this altarpiece.

14 DEATH AND THE MISER

Oil and tempera on panel. 36⅝ x 12¼″
National Gallery of Art, Washington, D. C.
(Samuel H. Kress Collection)

DEATH AS A PALE, skeleton-like figure enters the bedroom of a rich man and is ready to pierce him with his fatal arrow. It was common to show, in the so-called *artes moriendi* (handbooks on "the art of dying"), man, at his last hour, between the divine and the evil powers. In Bosch's version a devilish, frog-like monster has worked his way through the curtain of the death bed. He shows a money bag to the dying man, whereas an angel points out to him the image of the Saviour, which in the form of a tiny crucifix, is attached to the window at the upper left of the room. A beam of light shines through this window like a ray of Divine Grace. It forms a contrast to the little torch fire, symbol of the fire of hell, which is carried by a devil peering over the top of the canopy of the bed.

This choice of the dying man between the love of money and the love of God is only the last of the decisions man has had to make during his lifetime. The old man and the money chest which are depicted in front of the bed are a symbolic, didactic indication of what man is supposed to do. The chest inhabited and surrounded by demons is obviously a symbol of avarice. The old man bending over his hoarded treasures is shown in the act of renouncing this vice. He returns the gold to the chest where a demon is only too anxious to receive it.

The same idea is exemplified in the two groups of symbols in the foreground of the painting. The red coat thrown over the low stone wall and held by a devil can only have an evil meaning, whereas the various parts of an armor displayed at the right side form a contrast to the symbols at the left. The two groups undoubtedly symbolize avarice and generosity, using elements of the story of St. Martin who was a generous knight and gave away one part of his coat to a beggar. It is unquestionably this part of the coat which is depicted here as a symbol of avarice, since St. Martin did away with it in the same fashion in which a man renounces his sin.

15 THE SHIP OF FOOLS

Oil and tempera on panel. 22 x 12⅝″
The Louvre, Paris

THE SHIP OF FOOLS is a popular allegory often used in late medieval literature. The rudderless vessel, aimlessly drifting in the water with a crew of careless people, pictures the worldly life of the man whose thoughts are not directed toward the salvation of his soul.

The painting by Bosch shows a small boat overloaded with merry-makers and drifting in swampy waters, its mast jutting up into a dark, threatening sky. Bushes of green foliage are tied to the mast to characterize the voyage as a pleasure trip. The ship flies a pink pennant with a half moon signifying its sinful, heretic nature.

The fools in, and surrounding, the ship are shown in various occupations which appear as though chosen at random from daily life. Yet, here again, all the groups have a specific meaning as each of them symbolizes a particular sin. At the right, the drinking jester and the vomiting man are obviously meant to signify gluttony, while the group at the left with a woman hitting a man unquestionably pictures wrath. The fellow who climbs the mast with a knife ready to cut loose the goose probably depicts a game, but, at the same time, seems to symbolize greed. The man below him, with his face showing envious despair and with his arm outstretched toward the climber, possibly indicates envy; the sleeping face next to him may signify sloth. The place of prominence again is given to lust. This vice is depicted in the center by the lute-playing nun and the monk sitting at a table board which holds a dish of cherries indicating the couple's sinful sexual relations. They, too, are playing a game as they try to snatch a fritter dangling on a thread. The swimmers in front, probably additional illustrations of the same vice, accompany the ship on its dangerous trip.

There was another painting, now lost, showing the disastrous end of the voyage and the punishment of the sinners; such a work would be, to Bosch, the indispensable complement of a panel depicting the sins. The missing part probably represented the battered ship landing at the shores of hell.

16 THE TEMPTATION OF ST. ANTHONY

Oil and tempera on panel. 27½ x 20″
The Prado, Madrid

ACCORDING TO JOSÉ SIGÜENZA, writing about the year 1600, the devout and contemplative soul, such as that of St. Anthony, may be assisted by divine grace, in which event the things the Enemy presents to his outer and inner eye will not cause him anger or other irregular passions, nor move him from his purpose.

In this little panel, the good St. Anthony seems so untroubled and pensive that it might better have been entitled a *Meditation* than a *Temptation*. The Saint sits intimately with nature and appears to have reached a happy condition where the demons are small and even rather well disposed toward him. The companionable pig lying nearby is his familiar attribute. It is usually black, and in making it light, the painter probably intended to convey more strongly than any previous artist the idea that the good hermit had cleansed its porcine nature of all sensuality.

THE TITLE, SIZE, AND OTHER PERTINENT DATA ON THE PAINTINGS THAT FOLLOW,

WILL BE FOUND BY LIFTING EACH REPRODUCTION